party food

SNACKS, DIPS, AND NIBBLES
FOR SPECIAL OCCASIONS

LINDA DOESER

MAIN PHOTOGRAPHY BY IAN PARSONS

This is a Parragon Publishing Book
First published in 2003

Parragon Publishing
Queen Street House
4 Queen Street
Bath BA1 1HE, UK

Created and produced for Parragon by The Bridgewater Book Company Ltd.

Home economist Sara Hesketh

ISBN: 1-40540-629-1

Printed in China

NOTE

*This book uses imperial and metric measurements. Follow the same units of
measurement throughout; do not mix imperial and metric. All spoon measurements
are level: teaspoons are assumed to be 5 ml and tablespoons are assumed to be 15 ml.
Unless otherwise stated, milk is assumed to be whole milk, eggs and individual vegetables
such as potatoes are medium, and pepper is freshly ground black pepper.*

*The times given for each recipe are an approximate guide only because the preparation
times may differ according to the techniques used by different people and the cooking times may
vary as a result of the type of oven used. Ovens should be preheated to the specified temperature.
If using a fan-assisted oven, check the manufacturer's instructions for adjusting the time and
temperature. The preparation times include chilling and marinating times, where appropriate.*

*Recipes using raw or very lightly cooked eggs should be avoided by infants, the elderly,
pregnant women, convalescents, and anyone suffering from an illness.*

Contents

Introduction

Whether it is a long-planned celebration or an impromptu gathering, a party is always a uniquely special occasion. For the host, however, a party may also be a time of stress and hard work. Having to spend time ensuring that everyone is mingling, and that the conversation is flowing as freely as the drink, the last thing you need is to be worrying about the food that you are serving. It should be as

much fun to throw a party as it is to attend one. Only you can decide whether your guests will get on with each other or if you can afford to serve Champagne, but *Party Food* can at least take away any worries about what snacks to serve to keep your guests happy.

The book is divided into three chapters, all of which feature vegetarian as well as fish and meat recipes. So, no matter what the tastes of your guests, you can be sure to find dishes here to please everyone. Most of the recipes are for finger foods, which will minimize the amount of preparation and clearing up that you will need to do. As well as these, there are a few dishes that simply require a fork to

eat them. The emphasis throughout is on tasty treats that are easy to prepare. After all, we all want our guests to enjoy the food but don't want to spend so much time in the kitchen that we are too tired to enjoy ourselves.

The chapter on Dips & Pâtés offers a fabulous collection of recipes from around the world which are perfect for easy entertaining. Delicious treats range from Middle Eastern Baba Ghanoush (page 22) to Traditional English Potted Shrimp (page 32). All of these dishes are made in advance and can be laid out in a tempting array with a selection of different breads. Individual recipes provide specific serving suggestions, or you can try some of the party basics on page 6.

Cold Nibbles is the chapter to turn to for the main constituents of your buffet table. This chapter provides a wide choice of recipes for savory pastries

and cookies; stuffed and pickled vegetables; and tarts and nibbles. There are recipes for traditional favorites, such as Cheese Straws (page 46) and Sausage Rolls (page 70). For those with more exotic tastes, there is a selection of exciting and more unusual delicacies. These range from the spicy delight of Deep-fried Shrimp Balls (page 62) to the sunny flavor of Stuffed Grape Leaves (page 66). While all of these snacks are delicious cold, some can also be served warm or hot if you prefer.

The final chapter features a selection of Hot Nibbles. These are always a special treat, but it is easy to be over-ambitious, so the dishes in *Party Food* are nice and simple. Many of the recipes in this chapter are very speedy. Others can be prepared in advance, and then popped in the oven or broiled after your guests have arrived.

Whatever kind of party you are planning, from a family gathering to a New Year celebration, you will find the best bites and most moreish morsels for the occasion in this book. You can use the book to plan exactly what canapés and snacks will make the best combination for each event. Prepare everything well in advance, and you will be free to enjoy the party as much as your guests.

Essentials

Hosting a party, and making some tempting nibbles for your guests, should be fun. All you need is a selection of recipes, and some careful preparation.

Party Basics

Don't forget that there are plenty of ready-made nibbles that you can buy to increase the variety of your party snacks. Plain and flavored breadsticks, corn and tortilla chips, as well as plain potato chips, are great for dunking into homemade dips or just for nibbling on their own. Peanuts are party favorites, but you can also include cashew nuts, almonds, and pistachios. A selection of cheeses and a basket of crackers or crusty bread, served with a dish of butter, is easy and always popular.

If you are already planning to prepare a range of flavorsome foods, you can supplement them with some simpler snacks, such as broiled chicken drumsticks, sausages on sticks, and squares of toast with ready-made toppings such as lumpfish roe (red caviar), sliced hard-cooked eggs, smoked salmon, slices of salami, and soft cheese and chives. Garnish with herb sprigs, sliced stuffed olives, pearl onions, or tiny gherkins. Sandwiches, however, are best avoided as they quickly dry out.

If you don't mind providing cutlery as well as plates, you can also serve a selection of salads. Most supermarkets sell a wide selection of mixed leaf and vegetable salads that are ideal. Pasta and rice salads with a colorful mixture of drained canned corn kernels, red and yellow bell pepper strips, tomato wedges, cooked frozen peas and strips of ham are easily made and can be dressed with vinaigrette or mayonnaise.

Techniques

 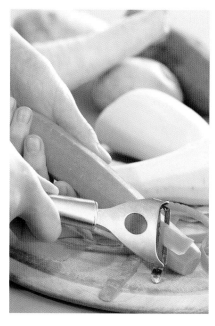

Crudités

Raw and blanched vegetables are perfect for serving with most dips and look very tempting on a large serving platter. Seed and slice red, yellow or orange bell peppers lengthwise. Baby corn cobs and trimmed, thin asparagus should be blanched in lightly salted boiling water. Include whole cherry tomatoes, small button mushrooms and trimmed radishes, perhaps with a few small leaves attached. Trim and separate the leaves of red and white chicory or the hearts of young Boston lettuces. Cut raw cauliflower into small florets and slice carrots, celery, and cucumber into sticks.

Vegetable Chips

Homemade vegetable chips make a delicious alternative to ordinary chips. You can, of course, use potatoes, but you might also like to try parsnips, carrots, or sweet potatoes. Peel the vegetables and slice very thinly using a mandoline or swivel-blade vegetable peeler. Heat sunflower or groundnut oil in a deep-fryer or large saucepan to 350–375°F/ 180–190°C, or until a cube of day-old bread browns in 30 seconds. Add the vegetable slices to the oil and fry until golden. Drain on paper towels and sprinkle with sea salt, paprika, or cayenne pepper. Store in an airtight container when cold.

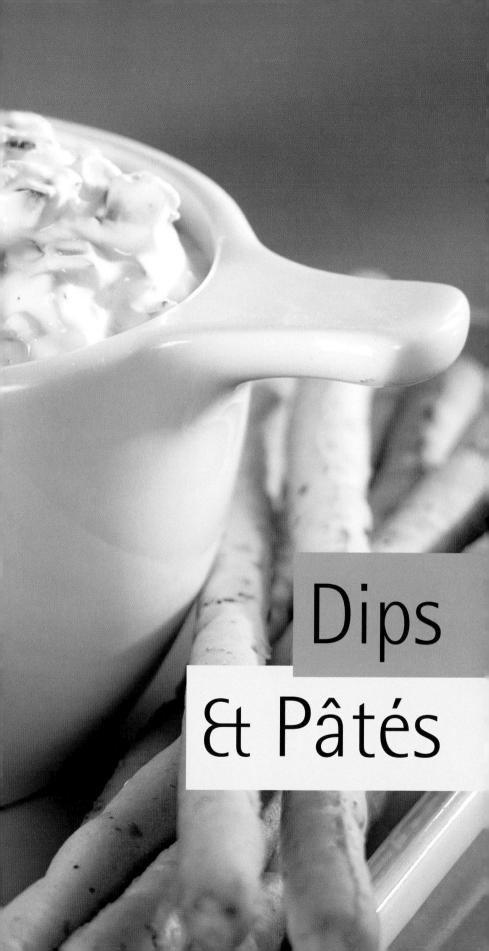

Dips

& Pâtés

Aïoli

This garlic mayonnaise from the Provence region of France is perfectly partnered with a selection of raw vegetables. It is reputed to keep flies away, so it would make the ideal choice for a summer buffet table.

serves 8

4 garlic cloves

salt

2 egg yolks

1 cup olive oil

lemon juice

pepper

To serve

Crudités (see page 7)

8 hard-cooked eggs, shelled

Method

❶ Place the garlic cloves and a pinch of salt in a glass bowl and crush with the back of a spoon. Add the egg yolks and beat briefly with an electric mixer until creamy.

❷ Add the oil, a few drops at a time, beating constantly with an electric mixer, until the mixture begins to thicken. Then add the remaining oil in a thin continuous stream, beating constantly.

❸ Stir in a little lemon juice to give the mayonnaise a dipping consistency. Season to taste with a little more salt, if necessary, and pepper. Cover with plastic wrap and store in the refrigerator until required.

❹ Before serving, return the aïoli to room temperature, if necessary, and transfer to a serving bowl. Arrange the Crudités on a large serving platter, arrange the eggs on top, and serve with the aïoli.

Tzatziki

This creamy Greek dip is very quick and easy to make, and is wonderfully refreshing on a hot summer's evening.

serves 8

1 cucumber

2 garlic cloves

8 scallions

2½ cups Greek-style (thick) yogurt

5 tbsp chopped fresh mint,
plus extra to garnish

salt and pepper

To serve

toasted mini pita breads

sesame breadsticks

Method

❶ Trim the cucumber, but do not peel. Cut it into small, neat dice. Finely chop the garlic and scallions.

❷ Beat the yogurt in a bowl with a fork until smooth, then fold in the cucumber, garlic, scallions, and mint. Season to taste with salt and pepper.

❸ Transfer to a serving bowl, cover with plastic wrap, and chill in the refrigerator until required. Serve with toasted mini pita breads and sesame breadsticks.

Taramasalata

Homemade taramasalata is infinitely tastier than anything you can buy at a delicatessen, so it is well worth the extra effort. It is traditionally made with gray mullet roe, but cod's roe is easier to find and just as good.

serves 8

8 oz/225 g (8–10 slices) stale white bread, crusts removed

12 oz/350 g smoked cod's roe

2 garlic cloves, chopped

2 slices onion

4 tbsp lemon juice

¾ cup olive oil

black Kalamata olives, to garnish

chunks of crusty bread, to serve

Method

❶ Coarsely tear up the bread and place it in a bowl. Add cold water to cover and set aside to soak for 10 minutes.

❷ Meanwhile, using a sharp knife, scrape the roe away from the thick outer skin. Place the roe in a food processor with the garlic, onion, and lemon juice. Drain the bread, squeeze out the excess water with your hands, and add it to the food processor. Process the mixture for 2 minutes, or until smooth.

❸ With the motor running, gradually add the oil through the feeder tube until the mixture is smooth and creamy. Scrape into a serving dish, cover with plastic wrap, and chill in the refrigerator until required.

❹ Garnish the taramasalata with the olives. Serve with chunks of crusty bread.

Guacamole

It is fortunate that this spicy Mexican dip is so speedy to prepare because you cannot make it too far in advance. If you do, the avocados will discolor.

serves 8

4 avocados	5 tbsp olive oil
2 garlic cloves	juice of 1½ limes
4 scallions	salt
3 fresh red chiles, seeded	chopped fresh cilantro leaves, to garnish
2 red bell peppers, seeded	tortilla chips, to serve

Method

❶ Cut the avocados in half lengthwise and twist the halves to separate. Remove and discard the stones and scoop the flesh into a large bowl with a spoon. Mash coarsely with a fork.

❸ Transfer the guacamole to a serving bowl. Drizzle the remaining oil over the top, sprinkle with the cilantro, and serve with tortilla chips.

❷ Finely chop the garlic, scallions, chiles, and peppers, then stir them into the mashed avocado. Add 4 tablespoons of the oil and the lime juice, season to taste with salt, and stir well to mix. If you prefer a smoother dip, process all the ingredients together in a food processor.

Red Bell Pepper Dip

Serving this pretty pale-pink dip on a platter of red and white vegetables makes it look especially appealing—but beware of the spicy kick.

serves 8

3 red bell peppers, halved and seeded

1 cup cream cheese

½ tsp cayenne pepper

salt

To serve

cherry tomatoes

radishes

radicchio leaves

celery stalks

cauliflower florets

white mushrooms, halved

Method

❶ Arrange the pepper halves, skin side up, on a baking sheet and place under a preheated hot broiler for 10–15 minutes until the skins begin to blacken and blister. Transfer to a plastic bag with tongs, tie the top, and set aside until the peppers are cool enough to handle.

❷ Remove the peppers from the bag and peel away the skins. Coarsely chop the flesh and place in a food processor. Process to a smooth purée, then scrape into a serving bowl.

❸ Stir in the cream cheese until smooth, then stir in the cayenne and salt to taste. Cover with plastic wrap and chill in the refrigerator until required.

❹ To serve, place the bowl in the center of a large platter and arrange the tomatoes, radishes, radicchio, celery, cauliflower, and mushrooms around it.

Hummus with Lebanese Seed Bread

Using canned chickpeas in this popular Middle Eastern dip saves time and effort when you are getting party food ready, but you could use dried chickpeas, soaked overnight and cooked in boiling water for about 2½ hours, or until tender.

serves 8

1½ cups canned chickpeas, drained and rinsed

1 cup tahini

4 garlic cloves

juice of 3 lemons

6 tbsp water

salt and ground black pepper

2 tbsp olive oil

2 tbsp chopped fresh flat-leaf parsley

Lebanese seed bread

½ cup toasted sesame seeds

½ cup poppy seeds

4 tbsp chopped fresh thyme

⅔ cup olive oil

6 pita breads

To garnish

cayenne pepper

black olives

Method

❶ For the bread, place the seeds and thyme in a mortar and crush lightly with a pestle. Stir in the oil. Gently split open the pita breads and brush the seed mixture over the cut sides. Cook under a preheated medium broiler until golden brown and crisp. Set aside to cool, then break into pieces. Store in an airtight container until required.

❷ Place the chickpeas, tahini, garlic, lemon juice, and 4 tablespoons of the water in a food processor. Process until smooth, adding the remaining water if necessary. Alternatively, thoroughly mash all the ingredients together in a bowl with a fork.

❸ Spoon the mixture into a serving dish and season to taste with salt and pepper. Make a shallow hollow in the top of the hummus and spoon in the oil. If you are not serving it immediately, cover with plastic wrap and store in the refrigerator until required.

❹ To serve, sprinkle the hummus with the parsley, dust lightly with cayenne, and garnish with black olives. Serve with the Lebanese Seed Bread.

Baba Ghanoush

This tasty eggplant dip is not so well known in the West as hummus
(see page 20), but is very popular in the Middle East.

serves 8

3 large eggplants

3 garlic cloves, chopped

6 tbsp tahini

6 tbsp lemon juice

1 tsp ground cumin

3 tbsp chopped fresh flat-leaf parsley

salt and ground black pepper

fresh flat-leaf parsley sprigs, to garnish

Vegetable Chips (see page 7), to serve

Method

❶ Prick the eggplants all over with a
fork and cut in half lengthwise. Arrange
the halves, skin side up, on a baking sheet
and place under a preheated low broiler
for 15 minutes, or until the skins begin to
blacken and blister and the flesh feels soft.
Remove from the heat and set aside until
cool enough to handle.

❷ Peel the eggplants and squeeze out
any excess moisture, then coarsely chop
the flesh and place in a food processor.
Add the garlic and 2 tablespoons of
the tahini and process to mix, then add
2 tablespoons of the lemon juice and
process again. Continue adding the tahini
and lemon juice alternately, processing
between each addition.

❸ When the mixture is smooth, scrape
it into a bowl and stir in the cumin and
chopped parsley. Season to taste with
salt and pepper.

❹ Transfer the dip to a serving dish. If you
are not serving it immediately, cover with
plastic wrap and chill in the refrigerator
until required. Return the dip to room
temperature to serve. Garnish with parsley
sprigs and serve with Vegetable Chips.

Quick Chicken Liver Pâté with Melba Toast

Although this is a speedy recipe, you need to leave time for the pâté to cool. If you like, make it up to three days in advance and chill, covered, in the refrigerator.

serves 8

2 tbsp olive oil

2 onions, chopped

2 garlic cloves, finely chopped

1 lb 8 oz/675 g chicken livers

3 tbsp brandy

2 tbsp chopped fresh parsley

1 tbsp chopped fresh sage

salt and pepper

1¼ cups cream cheese

fresh parsley sprigs, to garnish

Melba toast

8 slices medium-thick white bread

Method

❶ Heat the oil in a large, heavy-based skillet over a low heat. Add the onions and garlic and cook, stirring occasionally, for 5 minutes until softened.

❷ Add the livers and cook, stirring and turning occasionally, for 5 minutes, or until they are lightly browned and just beginning to crisp at the edges. Remove the pan from the heat, stir in the brandy, parsley, and sage, and season to taste with salt and pepper. Leave to cool slightly.

❸ Transfer the mixture to a food processor and process until smooth. You may need to scrape down the sides of the mixing bowl once or twice. Scrape the mixture into a bowl, cover with plastic wrap, and set aside to cool completely.

❹ Meanwhile, for the Melba Toast, lightly toast the bread on both sides under a preheated medium broiler. Cut off and discard the crusts, then slice each half to make two very thin slices, each with one untoasted side. Toast the uncooked sides of the bread until lightly golden and the edges begin to curl slightly. Remove from the broiler and set aside to cool. When completely cool, store in an airtight container until required.

❺ When the chicken liver mixture is cold, stir in the cream cheese until thoroughly combined. Cover with plastic wrap and chill in the refrigerator until required, but bring back to room temperature to serve. Garnish with parsley sprigs and serve with the Melba Toast.

Smoked Fish Pâté

British kippers are used here because they have such a rich flavor, provided that they have been hot smoked in the traditional way. You could also use whitefish or smoked mackerel, in which case omit the preliminary cooking in Step 1.

serves 8

900 g/2 lb undyed kippered herring fillets

2 garlic cloves, finely chopped

¾ cups olive oil

6 tbsp light cream

salt and ground black pepper

lemon slices, to garnish

crackers, to serve

Method

❶ Place the kippers in a large skillet or fish kettle and add cold water to just cover. Bring to a boil, then immediately reduce the heat and poach gently for 10 minutes until tender. If using a skillet, you may need to do this in batches.

❷ Transfer the fish to a cutting board using a fish slice. Remove and discard the skin. Coarsely flake the flesh with a fork and remove any remaining tiny bones. Transfer the fish to a pan and add the garlic. Place over a low heat and break up the fish with a wooden spoon.

❸ Gradually add the oil, beating well after each addition. Add the cream and beat until smooth, but do not allow the mixture to boil.

❹ Remove the pan from the heat and season to taste with salt, if necessary, and pepper. Spoon the pâté into a serving dish, cover and set aside to cool completely. Chill in the refrigerator until required (it can be refrigerated for up to 3 days).

❺ Garnish with lemon slices and serve with crackers.

Mushroom & Chestnut Pâté

This is a gloriously luxurious vegetarian party treat. Dried porcini are quite expensive, but they have a wonderfully intense flavor and you don't need many.

serves 8

8 oz/225 g dried chestnuts, soaked overnight

1 oz/25 g dried porcini mushrooms

4 tbsp hot water

4 tbsp Marsala or medium sherry

1 tbsp olive oil

1 lb 8 oz/675 g cremini or portabello mushrooms, sliced

1 tbsp balsamic vinegar

1 tbsp chopped fresh parsley

1 tbsp soy sauce

salt and ground black pepper

thinly sliced radish, to garnish

whole wheat toast triangles or crusty bread, to serve

Method

❶ Drain the chestnuts, place them in a pan, and add cold water to cover. Bring to a boil, then reduce the heat, cover, and simmer for 45 minutes, or until tender. Drain well and set aside to cool.

❷ Meanwhile, place the porcini in a small bowl with the hot water and 1 tablespoon of the Marsala. Set aside to soak for 20 minutes. Drain well, reserving the soaking liquid. Pat the mushrooms dry with paper towels. Strain the soaking liquid through a chinois or coffee filter paper.

❸ Heat the oil in a large, heavy-based skillet. Add the cremini mushrooms and cook over a low heat, stirring occasionally, for 5 minutes until softened.

❹ Add the porcini, the reserved soaking liquid, and the vinegar, and cook, stirring constantly, for 1 minute. Increase the heat and stir in the remaining Marsala. Cook, stirring frequently, for 3 minutes. Remove the pan from the heat.

❺ Transfer the chestnuts to a food processor and process to a purée. Add the mushroom mixture and parsley and process to a smooth paste. Add the soy sauce and salt and pepper to taste and briefly process again to mix.

❻ Scrape the pâté into a serving bowl, cover and chill in the refrigerator. Garnish with radish slices before serving and serve with toast triangles or crusty bread.

Cheese & Bean Pâté

This creamy pâté is based on classic Italian ingredients — ricotta and borlotti or cannellini beans, flavored with garlic, lemon juice, and flat-leaf parsley.

serves 8

1 lb 12 oz/800 g canned borlotti or
cannellini beans, drained and rinsed
1½ cups ricotta cheese
2 garlic cloves, coarsely chopped
4 tbsp lemon juice
4 oz/115 g butter, melted
3 tbsp chopped fresh flat-leaved parsley
salt and ground black pepper
sunflower oil, for greasing

To garnish
fresh flat-leaf parsley sprigs
lemon wedges

cheese-flavored focaccia fingers, to serve

Method

❶ Place the beans, ricotta, garlic, lemon juice, and melted butter in a food processor and process to a smooth purée. Add the chopped parsley and salt and pepper to taste and process again briefly to mix.

❷ Lightly oil a plain ring mold. Scrape the mixture into the mold and smooth the surface. Cover with plastic wrap and chill in the refrigerator until set.

❸ To serve, turn out the pâté on to a serving dish and fill the center with parsley sprigs. Garnish with lemon wedges and serve with focaccia fingers.

Traditional English Potted Shrimp

For authenticity, potted shrimp should be served with brown bread spread
with unsalted butter, but you could also serve them with whole wheat toast,
Melba Toast (see page 24) or even chunks of soda bread.

serves 8

10 oz/280 g unsalted butter

3 pieces of mace blade

pinch of freshly grated nutmeg

pinch of cayenne pepper

1 lb/450 g cooked peeled tiny shrimp

To garnish

fresh parsley sprigs

lemon slices

slices of brown bread, spread with unsalted
butter, to serve

Method

❶ Place 6 oz/175 g of the butter in a small, heavy-based pan and add the mace, nutmeg, and cayenne. Melt over the lowest possible heat, stirring occasionally.

❷ Add the shrimp and cook, stirring constantly, for 2 minutes, or until heated through. Do not allow the mixture to boil.

❸ Remove the pan from the heat, then remove and discard the mace. Spoon the mixture into a serving dish and level the surface. Cover and set aside to cool, then chill in the refrigerator until set. (Traditionally, potted shrimp are served in ramekins as individual appetizers. If you want to do this, divide the mixture equally between 8 small ramekins.)

❹ When the potted shrimp have set, place the remaining butter in a small, heavy-based pan. Melt over a low heat, then skim off the scum that has formed on the surface. Carefully pour off the clear liquid into a bowl, leaving the white milk solids in the base of the pan. Spoon the clarified butter over the top of the potted shrimp to make a thin, covering layer. Cover and return to the refrigerator until set.

❺ Garnish the potted shrimp with parsley sprigs and lemon slices and serve with the buttered slices of bread.

Cold

Nibbles

Three-Flavor Pinwheels

These tasty little morsels look so appetizing that your guests are sure to snap them up with delight.

makes 50–60

Ham and cream cheese pinwheels
¾ cup cream cheese

4 large slices lean ham

4 tbsp snipped fresh chives

Beef and horseradish pinwheels
½ cup heavy double cream

2 tbsp creamed horseradish

4 large slices medium-rare roast beef

Smoked salmon and dill cream pinwheels
1 cup heavy cream

2 tbsp chopped fresh dill

ground black pepper

4 large or 8 medium slices smoked salmon

4 tbsp lemon juice

Method

❶ For the Ham and Cream Cheese Pinwheels, spread the cream cheese evenly over the slices of ham. Sprinkle with the chives. Roll up each slice tightly and wrap individually in plastic wrap. Chill in the refrigerator for 1 hour.

❷ For the Beef and Horseradish Pinwheels, whip the cream in a bowl until stiff, then fold in the creamed horseradish. Spread the mixture evenly over the slices of beef. Roll up each slice tightly and wrap individually in plastic wrap. Chill in the refrigerator for 1 hour.

❸ For the Smoked Salmon and Dill Cream Pinwheels, whip the cream in a bowl until stiff, then fold in the dill and pepper to taste. Spread the mixture evenly over the slices of smoked salmon. Roll up each slice tightly and wrap individually in plastic wrap. Chill in the refrigerator for 1 hour.

❹ When ready to serve, unwrap the rolls one at a time and thinly slice. Before slicing the Smoked Salmon and Dill Cream Pinwheels, sprinkle with a little lemon juice. Impale each pinwheel on a wooden toothpick and arrange on a serving platter.

Garlic & Chive Crackers

These crumbly, flavor-packed savory crackers are ideal for serving on their own or with a selection of cheeses.

makes 25

4 tbsp unsalted butter, softened, plus extra for greasing

2 tbsp finely snipped fresh chives

scant 1 cup all-purpose flour, plus extra for dusting

2 tbsp freshly grated Parmesan cheese

1 egg yolk

2–3 tbsp ice water

3 garlic cloves, finely chopped

1 egg yolk, beaten, to glaze

Method

❶ Using a wooden spoon or a fork, beat the butter with the chives in a bowl until thoroughly combined.

❷ Sift the flour into a bowl and stir in the Parmesan. Add the chive butter and rub it in with your fingertips until the mixture resembles bread crumbs. Add the egg yolk and enough of the water to make a soft dough. Shape the dough into a ball, wrap in foil and chill in the refrigerator for 30 minutes.

❸ Preheat the oven to 400°F/200°C. Grease a cookie sheet with a little butter. Unwrap the dough and roll out on a lightly floured counter. Sprinkle the garlic evenly over the dough, then fold it in half and roll out thinly again. Stamp out rounds using a 2½-inch/6-cm fluted cutter.

❹ Place the rounds on the cookie sheet and brush with the beaten egg to glaze. Bake in the preheated oven for 15–20 minutes, or until golden. Remove from the oven and cool for a few minutes. Transfer to a wire rack to cool completely. Store in an airtight container until required.

Egg & Tapenade Toasties

Tapenade is a black olive, caper, and anchovy paste from Provence. It goes especially well with hard-cooked eggs, but you could also top these toasties with flaked canned tuna.

makes 8

1 small French loaf

4 tomatoes, thinly sliced

4 eggs, hard-cooked

4 bottled or canned anchovy fillets in olive oil, drained and halved lengthwise

8 marinated pitted black olives

few fine frisée leaves, to garnish (optional)

Tapenade

1 cup chopped black olives

6 bottled or canned anchovy fillets in olive oil, drained

2 tbsp capers, rinsed

2 garlic cloves, coarsely chopped

1 tsp Dijon mustard

2 tbsp lemon juice

1 tsp fresh thyme leaves

ground black pepper

4–5 tbsp olive oil

Method

❶ For the Tapenade, place the olives, anchovies, capers, garlic, mustard, lemon juice, thyme, and pepper to taste in a food processor and process for 20–25 seconds, or until smooth. Scrape down the sides of the mixing bowl, then with the motor running, gradually add the oil through the feeder tube to make a smooth paste. Spoon the paste into a bowl, cover with plastic wrap, and set aside until required.

❷ Cut the French loaf into 8 slices, discarding the crusty ends. Toast on both sides under a preheated medium broiler until light golden brown. Leave to cool.

❸ To assemble the toasties, spread a little of the tapenade on one side of each slice of toast. Top with the tomato slices. Shell the eggs, then slice and arrange over the tomatoes. Dot a little of the remaining tapenade on each egg slice. Wind the anchovy fillets around the egg slices in an "S" shape. Halve the marinated olives and arrange 2 halves on each toasty. Garnish with the frisée leaves and serve.

Filled Croustades

Much more fun than sandwiches—and less likely to become dry and unappetizing—
these crisp containers go well with an endless variety of easy-to-make fillings. In
addition to those below, scrambled eggs topped with slivers of ham or salami and
cucumber; Smoked Fish Pâté (see page 26), garnished with sliced stuffed olives; or
Guacamole (see page 16), topped with chopped tomato and pickled jalapeño
chiles, would work well.

makes 48

Croustades	Crab salad filling
1 lb 5 oz/600 g butter	4 oz/115 g crabmeat, drained if canned
12 large slices white bread	and thawed if frozen
	½ cup mayonnaise
Cheese & tomato filling	pinch of celery salt
Tapenade (see page 40)	2 eggs, hard-cooked
mozzarella cheese, thinly sliced	fresh dill sprigs, to garnish
cherry tomatoes, halved	
fresh basil leaves, to garnish	

Method

❶ Preheat the oven to 350°F/180°C. Make the croustades in four batches. Melt one-quarter of the butter in a heavy-based pan over a low heat. Meanwhile, stamp out 12 rounds of bread with a 7.5-cm/3-inch fluted cookie cutter. When the butter has melted, remove the pan from the heat. Dip the bread rounds into the melted butter and press them firmly into the cups of a muffin pan.

❷ Place a second muffin pan on top to keep the bread rounds in shape. Bake in the preheated oven for 15–20 minutes, or until the croustades are crisp and firm. Transfer to a wire rack to cool completely while you cook the remaining batches. When the croustades are cold, fill with your chosen filling and serve.

❸ For the Cheese and Tomato Filling, spoon Tapenade into the croustades, top each one with a slice of mozzarella and a tomato half, and garnish with a basil leaf.

❹ For the Crab Salad Filling, place the crabmeat in a bowl and flake with a fork. Stir in the mayonnaise and celery salt. Shell the eggs, finely chop, and stir into the filling mixture. Spoon into the croustades and garnish with dill sprigs.

Easy Nibbles

Lots of different flavors and textures, and food that is easy to handle and eat, are the keys to party success. This duo of tasty treats satisfies all those criteria.

makes 40

Celery & endive boats	Deviled eggs
2 cups cream cheese	6 hard-cooked eggs, shelled
4 scallions, finely chopped	2 scallions, finely chopped
4 tbsp chopped sun-dried tomatoes in oil	6 walnut halves, finely chopped
3 tbsp chopped fresh parsley	1 tbsp mayonnaise
1 tbsp snipped fresh chives	2 fresh green chiles, seeded and
1 cup chopped pimiento-stuffed olives	finely chopped
1 tbsp Tabasco sauce	1 tbsp Dijon mustard
2 heads Belgian endive, separated	1 tsp white wine vinegar
into leaves	cayenne pepper
12 celery stalks	salt and pepper
fine strips of red bell pepper, to garnish	thinly sliced baby gherkins, to garnish

Method

❶ For the Celery & Endive Boats, beat the cream cheese in a bowl with a wooden spoon until smooth. Stir in the scallions, sun-dried tomatoes, parsley, chives, olives, and Tabasco and mix well. Spoon the mixture into the hollows of the Belgian endive leaves and celery stalks and arrange on a serving plate. Garnish with the strips of red bell pepper.

❷ For the Deviled Eggs, cut the eggs in half lengthwise and scoop out the yolks into a bowl without piercing the whites. Mash the yolks well with a fork, then mix in the scallions, walnuts, mayonnaise, chiles, mustard, and vinegar. Season to taste with cayenne, salt, and pepper. Spoon the mixture into the egg white halves and garnish with gherkin slices.

Cheese Straws

Nothing could be simpler or more popular than freshly made cheese straws. You can make the dough in advance, bake one batch, and store the remainder, wrapped in foil in the refrigerator, to bake during the party and replenish supplies.

makes 60

scant 2 cups all purpose flour, plus extra
for dusting

salt and ground black pepper

cayenne pepper

mustard powder

4 oz/115 g butter, diced, plus extra
for greasing

¾ cup freshly grated Parmesan or
pecorino cheese

2 egg yolks

1–2 tbsp cold water (optional)

1 egg white, lightly beaten, to glaze

Method

❶ Sift the flour into a bowl with a pinch each of salt, pepper, cayenne, and mustard powder. Add the butter and rub it in with your fingertips until the mixture resembles bread crumbs. Stir in the cheese. Add the egg yolks and mix well, adding a little of the cold water, as required, to bind. Shape the dough into a ball.

❷ Preheat the oven to 425°F/220°C. Roll out the dough on a lightly floured counter to about ½-inch/1-cm thick. Using a sharp knife, cut it into fingers and arrange on greased cookie sheets, spaced slightly apart. Brush with the egg white.

❸ Bake in the preheated oven for 8–10 minutes, or until golden brown. Remove from the oven and leave to cool on the cookie sheets. When completely cool, store in an airtight container, but they are best served as fresh as possible.

Quiche Lorraine

This elegant version of the classic French egg and bacon tart is delicious as it is, or can form the basis of an even more elaborate quiche. You can, for example, arrange cooked or canned asparagus spears in a wheel on the top, or smother it with a layer of lightly sautéed mushrooms.

makes 9-inch/1 x 23-cm quiche

Pastry

scant 1½ cups all-purpose flour, plus extra
for dusting

pinch of salt

4 oz/115 g butter, diced

¼ cup freshly grated pecorino cheese

4–6 tbsp ice water

Filling

1 cup thinly sliced Gruyère cheese

½ cup crumbled Roquefort cheese

6 oz/175 g rindless lean bacon,
broiled until crisp

3 eggs

⅔ cup heavy cream

salt and pepper

Method

❶ To make the pastry, sift the flour with the salt into a bowl. Add the butter and rub it in with your fingertips until the mixture resembles bread crumbs. Stir in the grated cheese, then stir in enough of the water to bind. Shape the dough into a ball, wrap in foil, and chill in the refrigerator for 15 minutes.

❷ Preheat the oven to 375°F/190°C. Unwrap and roll out the dough on a lightly floured counter. Use to line a 9-inch/23-cm quiche pan. Place the pan on a cookie sheet. Prick the base of the pastry case all over with a fork, line with foil or parchment paper, and fill with baking beans. Bake in the preheated oven for 15 minutes until the edges are set and dry.

Remove the beans and lining and bake the pastry case for a further 5–7 minutes, or until golden. Leave to cool slightly.

❸ For the filling, arrange the cheese over the base of the pastry case, then crumble the bacon evenly on top. In a bowl, beat the eggs with the cream until thoroughly combined. Add salt and pepper to taste. Pour the mixture into the pastry case and return to the oven for 20 minutes, or until the filling is golden and set.

❹ Remove from the oven and cool the quiche in the pan for 10 minutes. Transfer to a wire rack to cool completely. Cover and store in the refrigerator, but return to room temperature before serving.

Moroccan Pickled Vegetables

Snacking is an art form in North Africa, so it is well worth adopting their clever ideas to serve as flavorful party food.

serves 12

24 small radishes

24 baby carrots

8 celery stalks

1 cucumber

salt and pepper

3½ oz/100 g superfine sugar

4 fl oz/125 ml lemon juice

2 tbsp pink peppercorns

1 bunch of fresh cilantro, finely chopped

Method

❶ Place the radishes and carrots in a large, nonmetallic bowl. Cut the celery stalks into 2-inch/5-cm lengths and add to the bowl. Halve the cucumber lengthwise, scoop out the seeds with a teaspoon and discard, then thickly slice and add to the bowl. Sprinkle the vegetables generously with salt, cover with plastic wrap, and set aside for 3–4 hours.

❷ Tip the vegetables into a colander and rinse thoroughly under cold running water to remove all traces of salt. Drain well and pat dry with paper towels. Transfer the vegetables to a nonmetallic bowl.

❸ In a separate nonmetallic bowl, mix together the sugar, lemon juice, and peppercorns, stirring until the sugar has completely dissolved. Season to taste with pepper.

❹ Pour the dressing over the vegetables and toss gently to mix. Cover with plastic wrap and chill for 8 hours or overnight in the refrigerator.

❺ Just before serving, stir in the chopped cilantro, then transfer to a serving dish. Serve chilled with a supply of wooden toothpicks for spearing the vegetables.

Böreks

These crisp, cheese-filled pastries are a Turkish specialty, although they are popular throughout the Middle East. They are traditionally made with sheep milk cheese, but you could substitute grated Gruyère if you prefer.

makes 20

8 oz/225 g feta cheese (drained weight)

2 tbsp chopped fresh mint

2 tbsp chopped fresh parsley

1½ tbsp chopped fresh dill

pinch of freshly grated nutmeg

ground black pepper

20 sheets phyllo pastry (about

4½ x 7 inches/12 x 18 cm), thawed

if frozen

olive oil, for brushing

Method

❶ Crumble the feta into a bowl and add the mint, parsley, dill, and nutmeg. Season to taste with pepper and mix thoroughly.

❷ Preheat the oven to 375°F/190°C. Keep the phyllo pastry sheets covered with plastic wrap to prevent them from drying out. Take a sheet of phyllo and brush with oil. Place a second sheet on top and brush with oil. Cut in half lengthwise. Place a teaspoon of the cheese mixture at the short end of one long strip, fold in the corners diagonally, and roll up. Brush the end with a little oil to seal and place, seam side down, on a cookie sheet. Repeat with the remaining sheets of phyllo and filling.

❸ Brush the tops of the pastries with a little more oil and bake in the preheated oven for 15–20 minutes, or until golden and crisp. Remove from the oven and transfer to a wire rack to cool. Serve at room temperature. The Böreks can also be deep-fried.

Little Feta & Spinach Crescents

The traditional recipe for spanakopita, a famous Greek pie, has been adapted to make these attractive, melt-in-the mouth crescents.

makes 16

1 lb/450 g spinach, coarse stalks removed

4 scallions, finely chopped

2 eggs, lightly beaten

1 tbsp chopped fresh parsley

1 tbsp chopped fresh dill

12 oz/350 g feta cheese (drained weight)

pepper

8 sheets phyllo pastry (about 4½ x 7 inches/ 12 x 18 cm), thawed if frozen

olive oil, for brushing

Method

❶ Pour water to a depth of about ½ inch/ 1 cm into a large pan and bring to a boil. Add the spinach and cook, turning once, for 1–2 minutes, until just wilted. Drain well, then squeeze out as much excess liquid as you can with your hands. Finely chop the spinach and place in a large bowl. Add the scallions, eggs, parsley, and dill. Crumble in the feta and season to taste with pepper. Mix together thoroughly.

❷ Preheat the oven to 375°F/190°C. Keep the phyllo pastry sheets covered with plastic wrap to prevent them from drying out. Take a sheet of phyllo, brush with oil, and cut in half lengthwise. Spread a little of the filling across one corner, leaving a small margin on either side. Roll up securely but not too tightly and curl in the ends to make a crescent shape. Place on a cookie sheet. Repeat with the remaining sheets of phyllo and filling.

❸ Brush the crescents with oil and bake in the preheated oven for 25 minutes until golden and crisp. Remove from the oven and leave on the cookie sheet for 5 minutes, then transfer to a wire rack to cool. Serve at room temperature.

Cheese & Apricot Morsels

These unusual little snacks make an eye-catching addition to a buffet table, yet are very easy and quick to make.

makes 20

1 cup cream cheese

6 tbsp milk

1 cup finely grated sharp mature Cheddar cheese

salt and ground black pepper

1 lb 12 oz/800 g canned apricot halves in juice, drained

To garnish

about 20 walnut pieces

paprika

Method

❶ Beat the cream cheese in a bowl with a wooden spoon until softened. Gradually beat in the milk and Cheddar. Season to taste with salt and pepper.

❷ Spoon the cheese mixture into a pastry bag fitted with a ½-inch/1-cm star tip. Pipe swirls of the mixture into the hollow side of each apricot half.

❸ Arrange the filled apricot halves in a serving dish, then top each with a piece of walnut and dust lightly with a little paprika to garnish.

Caribbean Crab Cakes

These spicy snacks are delicious served warm as well as cold and go well with the
Red Bell Pepper Dip (see page 18) or Spicy Salsa (see page 76).

makes 16

1 potato, cut into chunks	½ tsp Dijon mustard
pinch of salt	½ fresh green chile, seeded and
4 scallions, chopped	finely chopped
1 garlic clove, chopped	1 egg, lightly beaten
1 tbsp chopped fresh thyme	ground black pepper
1 tbsp chopped fresh basil	all-purpose flour, for dusting
1 tbsp chopped fresh cilantro	sunflower oil, for frying
8 oz/225 g white crabmeat, drained if	lime wedges, to garnish
canned and thawed if frozen	dip or salsa of choice, to serve

Method

❶ Place the potato in a small pan and add water to cover. Add the salt. Bring to a boil, then reduce the heat, cover and simmer for 10-15 minutes, or until softened. Drain well, turn into a large bowl, and mash with a potato masher or fork until smooth.

❷ Meanwhile, place the scallions, garlic, thyme, basil, and cilantro in a mortar and pound with a pestle until smooth. Add the herb paste to the mashed potato with the crabmeat, mustard, chile, egg, and pepper to taste. Mix well, cover with plastic wrap, and chill in the refrigerator for 30 minutes.

❸ Sprinkle flour on to a shallow plate. Shape spoonfuls of the crabmeat mixture into small balls with your hands, then flatten slightly and dust with flour, shaking off any excess. Heat the oil in a skillet over a high heat, add the crab cakes, in batches, and cook for 2-3 minutes on each side until golden. Remove from the pan and drain on paper towels. Set aside to cool to room temperature.

❹ Arrange the crab cakes on a serving dish and garnish with lime wedges. Serve with a bowl of dip or salsa.

Anchovy, Olive & Cheese Triangles

Ideal for parties, these fabulous little Spanish tapas can be made in advance and stored in an airtight container. If you can't find Manchego cheese, substitute sharp Cheddar.

makes 40

2 oz/55 g canned anchovy fillets in olive oil, drained and coarsely chopped

½ cup oz coarsely chopped black olives

1 cup finely grated Manchego cheese

scant 1 cup all-purpose flour, plus extra for dusting

4 oz/115 g unsalted butter, diced

½ tsp cayenne pepper, plus extra for dusting

Method

❶ Place the anchovies, olives, cheese, flour, butter, and cayenne in a food processor and pulse until a dough forms. Turn out and shape into a ball. Wrap in foil and chill in the refrigerator for 30 minutes.

❷ Preheat the oven to 400°F/200°C. Unwrap the dough, knead on a lightly floured counter, and roll out thinly. Using a sharp knife, cut it into strips about 2-inches/5-cm wide. Cut diagonally across each strip, turning the knife in alternate directions, to make triangles.

❸ Arrange the triangles on 2 cookie sheets and dust lightly with cayenne pepper. Bake in the preheated oven for 10 minutes, or until golden brown. Transfer to wire racks to cool completely.

Deep-Fried Shrimp Balls

These spicy Indonesian snacks are very moreish and are just as delicious served hot. Sambal oelek is a fiery hot paste made from chiles. It is available from large supermarkets and Chinese food stores.

makes 25

10 oz/280 g raw shrimp,
peeled and deveined

1-inch/2.5-cm piece fresh gingerroot,
coarsely chopped

2½ cups beans prouts, coarsely chopped

1 bunch of scallions,
coarsely chopped

scant 1 cup all-purpose flour

1 tsp baking powder

1 egg, lightly beaten

½ tsp sambal oelek

pinch of salt

1–2 tbsp lukewarm water (optional)

groundnut or sunflower oil,
for deep-frying

dip of choice, to serve (optional)

Method

❶ Place the shrimp, ginger, bean sprouts, and scallions in a food processor and process until finely chopped, scraping down the sides of the mixing bowl once or twice. Scrape the mixture into a bowl and add the flour, baking powder, egg, sambal oelek, and salt. Mix thoroughly with your hands until a firm mixture forms, adding a little of the water if necessary.

❷ Heat the oil in a deep-fryer or large pan to 350–375°F/180–190°C, or until a cube of day-old bread browns in 30 seconds.

❸ Meanwhile, shape spoonfuls of the shrimp mixture into walnut-sized balls with your hands. Add the shrimp balls to the hot oil in batches, and deep-fry for 2–3 minutes until golden brown. Remove with a slotted spoon and drain on paper towels. If serving hot, serve immediately, or leave to cool to room temperature. Serve with a dip, if desired.

Sicilian Shrimp

This attractive dish makes a lovely centerpiece for a buffet table, but you will need to provide plates and forks for your guests.

serves 12

salt

2¾ cups long-grain rice

3 tbsp white wine vinegar

1 tsp Dijon mustard

2 garlic cloves

⅔ cups olive oil

paprika

1¾ cups mayonnaise

juice of 3 oranges

juice of ½ lemon

3 shallots, finely chopped

2 cups crushed tomatoes

1 lb/450 g cooked peeled shrimp

1 cup slivered almonds

sunflower oil, for greasing

fresh parsley sprigs, to garnish

Method

❶ Bring a large pan of lightly salted water to a boil. Add the rice and return to a boil. Reduce the heat and simmer for 15 minutes, or until tender. Drain well, rinse under cold running water, then drain again and set aside to cool completely.

❷ Mix together the vinegar and mustard in a nonmetallic bowl. Place the garlic on a cutting board and smash with the side of a large, heavy knife. Sprinkle over a little salt and finely chop. Add the garlic to the vinegar mixture and mix well, then gradually whisk in the oil until the dressing has thickened. Season and lightly color with paprika. Set aside.

❸ In a separate bowl, mix together the mayonnaise, orange juice, lemon juice, shallots, and tomatoes. Gently fold in the shrimp. Cover with plastic wrap and set aside in the refrigerator until required.

❹ When the rice is cold, add the dressing and stir in the almonds. Spoon the rice mixture into a lightly oiled round mold, cover with plastic wrap, and chill in the refrigerator for at least 30 minutes.

❺ To serve, turn out the rice on to a large serving plate, carefully scoop out the center, and spoon the shrimp mixture into the hollow. Garnish with parsley sprigs.

Stuffed Grape Leaves

With all the sunny flavors of Greece, these vegetarian parcels are perfect for a summer party.

serves 12

salt

2 cups long-grain rice

1 lb/450 g grape leaves, rinsed if preserved in brine

2 onions, finely chopped

1 bunch of scallions, finely chopped

1 bunch of fresh parsley, finely chopped

½ cup finely chopped fresh mint

1 tbsp fennel seeds

1 tsp crushed dried chiles

finely grated rind of 2 lemons

1 cup olive oil

2½ cups boiling water

lemon wedges, to garnish

Tzatziki (see page 12), to serve

Method

❶ Bring a large pan of lightly salted water to a boil. Add the rice and return to a boil. Reduce the heat and simmer for 15 minutes, or until tender.

❷ Meanwhile, if using preserved grape leaves, place them in a heatproof bowl and pour over boiling water to cover. Set aside to soak for 10 minutes. If using fresh grape leaves, bring a pan of water to the boil, add the grape leaves, then reduce the heat and simmer for 10 minutes.

❸ Drain the rice and, while still hot, mix with the onions, scallions, parsley, mint, fennel seeds, chiles, lemon rind, and 3 tablespoons of the oil in a large bowl. Season to taste with salt.

❹ Drain the grape leaves well. Spread out 1 leaf, vein side up, on a counter. Place a generous teaspoonful of the rice mixture on the leaf near the stalk. Fold the stalk end over the filling, fold in the sides, and roll up the leaf. Repeat until all the filling has been used. There may be some grape leaves left over—you can use them to line a serving platter, if you like.

❺ Place the parcels in a large, heavy-based pan in a single layer (you may need to use 2 pans). Spoon over the remaining oil, then add the boiling water. Cover the parcels with an inverted heatproof plate to keep them below the surface of the water, cover the pan and simmer for 1 hour.

❻ Allow the parcels to cool to room temperature in the pan, then transfer to a serving platter with a slotted spoon. Garnish with lemon wedges and serve with Tzatziki.

Vegetable Samosas

These aromatic Indian snacks are always popular and taste good served hot or cold. You can make them in advance and freeze them ready to cook or to serve after thawing.

makes 30

3 large potatoes, cut into chunks

salt

¾ cup frozen peas

½ cup frozen corn kernels, thawed

2 shallots, finely chopped

1 tsp ground cumin

1 tsp ground coriander

2 fresh green chiles, seeded and finely chopped

2 tbsp chopped fresh mint

2 tbsp chopped fresh cilantro

4 tbsp lemon juice

15 sheets phyllo pastry (about 4½ x 7 inches/12 x 18 cm), thawed if frozen

melted butter, for brushing

groundnut or sunflower oil, for deep-frying

mango chutney, to serve

Method

❶ Place the potatoes in a pan and add cold water to cover and a pinch of salt. Bring to a boil, then reduce the heat, cover, and simmer for 15–20 minutes until tender. Meanwhile, cook the peas according to the instructions on the package. Drain and transfer to a bowl. Drain the potatoes, return to the pan, and mash coarsely with a potato masher or fork. Add them to the peas.

❷ Add the corn, shallots, cumin, ground coriander, chiles, mint, fresh cilantro, and lemon juice, and season to taste with salt. Mix well.

❸ Keep the phyllo pastry sheets covered with plastic wrap to prevent them from drying out. Take a sheet of phyllo, brush with melted butter, and cut in half lengthwise. Place a tablespoonful of the filling at one end of a strip. Fold over a corner to make a triangle and roll up the pastry strip. Repeat with the remaining sheets of phyllo and filling.

❹ Heat the oil in a deep-fryer or large pan to 350–375°F/180–190°C, or until a cube of day-old bread browns in 30 seconds. Add the samosas in batches, and cook until golden brown. Remove with a slotted spoon and drain on kitchen paper. Alternatively, bake the samosas in a preheated oven, 400°F/200°C, for 10–15 minutes until golden brown. Serve hot or at room temperature with mango chutney.

Sausage Rolls

Homemade sausage rolls are so much tastier than the store-bought variety, especially if you can buy good-quality sausagemeat. They are very easy to make and can be served warm or cold.

makes 48

1 lb/450 g sausagemeat

1 tsp Worcestershire sauce

beaten egg, to glaze

Pastry

scant 2 cups all-purpose flour,
plus extra for dusting

pinch of salt

½ tsp mustard powder

4 oz/115 g butter, diced

2–3 tbsp ice water

Method

❶ For the pastry, sift the flour into a bowl with the salt and mustard powder. Add the butter and rub it in with your fingertips until the mixture resembles bread crumbs. Gradually stir in enough of the water to make a soft, but not sticky, dough. Shape the dough into a ball, wrap in foil, and chill in the refrigerator for 20 minutes.

❷ Mix together the sausagemeat and Worcestershire sauce in a bowl until thoroughly combined and the meat is broken up. Divide the mixture into 12 portions and roll each one between the palms of your hands to make a 6-inch/15-cm long sausage.

❸ Preheat the oven to 375°F/190°C. Roll out the dough on a lightly floured counter to a rectangle measuring 8 x 18 inches/20 x 45 cm. Using a sharp knife, cut the dough into 12 rectangles, each measuring about 2 x 6 inches/5 x 15 cm. Place a sausagemeat roll on a dough rectangle and brush the long edges of the dough with water. Carefully roll the pastry over the sausagemeat to enclose it, then cut the roll into 4 equal pieces. Repeat with the remaining dough and sausagemeat rolls.

❹ Arrange the sausage rolls on 2 cookie sheets, seam side down. Brush with the beaten egg and bake in the preheated oven for 10 minutes, or until golden brown and cooked through. Remove from the oven and transfer the sausage rolls to a wire rack to cool.

Honey & Mustard Drumsticks

Chicken drumsticks make good party food as they are so easy to eat with the fingers. This sweet and sour marinade makes them completely irresistible.

makes 12

12 chicken drumsticks

6 tbsp clear honey

6 tbsp wholegrain mustard

2 tbsp Dijon mustard

2 tbsp white wine vinegar

3 tbsp sunflower oil

fresh parsley sprigs, to garnish

Method

❶ Using a sharp knife, make several slashes in each drumstick, then place them in a large, nonmetallic dish.

❷ Mix together the honey, both types of mustard, vinegar, and oil in a pitcher, whisking well to combine. Pour the marinade over the chicken, turning and stirring to coat. Cover with plastic wrap and set aside in the refrigerator to marinate for at least 2–3 hours or overnight.

❸ Place the drumsticks on a broiler rack and cook under a preheated medium broiler, turning and brushing frequently with the marinade, for 25 minutes, or until the chicken is tender and the juices run clear when a skewer is inserted into the thickest part of the meat. Set aside to cool, then arrange on a serving platter and garnish with parsley sprigs.

Hot
Nibbles

Spicy Seafood Kabobs

These tempting shrimp and angler fish skewers are perfect for parties because they take only a few minutes to cook.

makes 8

2 tsp grated fresh gingerroot

2 garlic cloves, finely chopped

2 fresh green chiles, seeded and finely chopped

2 tbsp groundnut or sunflower oil

3 lb 5 oz/1.5 kg angler fish fillet, cut into 24 chunks

8 raw tiger shrimp, peeled and tails left intact

salt and ground black pepper

Spicy salsa

2 tomatoes

4 Scotch bonnet chiles

4 green jalapeño chiles, seeded and finely chopped

2 tbsp chopped fresh cilantro

2 tbsp olive oil

1 tbsp red wine vinegar

salt

Method

❶ Mix together the ginger, garlic, green chiles, and groundnut oil in a large, nonmetallic bowl. Add the angler fish chunks and shrimp and stir well to coat. Cover with plastic wrap and set aside in the refrigerator to marinate for 1 hour.

❷ Meanwhile, for the salsa, cut a small cross in the bottom of each tomato, place in a heatproof bowl, and pour over boiling water to cover. Leave for 30 seconds until the skins begin to peel back. Drain and, when cool enough to handle, peel.

❸ Place the Scotch bonnet chiles on a cookie sheet and cook under a preheated medium broiler, turning frequently, until the skin blackens and blisters. Transfer to a plastic bag with tongs and tie the top.

❹ Place the chopped chiles in a bowl. Scoop out and discard the tomato seeds, finely chop the flesh, and add to the bowl. Remove the Scotch bonnet chiles from the bag and peel away the skins. Halve them, discard the seeds, and finely chop the flesh. (Wear rubber gloves to protect your hands as they are very hot.) Add them to the bowl with the cilantro. Whisk the oil with the vinegar in a small bowl and season to taste with salt. Pour over the salsa, cover with plastic wrap, and chill in the refrigerator until required.

❺ Thread the seafood on to 8 skewers. Cook under a preheated hot broiler, turning frequently, for 6–8 minutes, or until cooked and tender. Transfer to a serving dish, season, and serve with the salsa.

Seafood Phyllo Parcels

These decorative, crisp phyllo pastry parcels are filled with succulent salmon and tasty crabmeat.

makes 24

3½ oz/100g canned red salmon, drained

3½ oz/100g canned crabmeat, drained

2 tbsp chopped fresh parsley

8 scallions, finely chopped

8 sheets phyllo pastry (about 8 x 12 inches/20 x 30 cm), thawed if frozen

melted butter, for brushing

sunflower oil, for greasing

Method

❶ Remove and discard the skin and bones from the salmon, place in a bowl, and flake the flesh with a fork. Remove and discard any cartilage from the crabmeat, place in another bowl, and flake gently with a fork. Divide the parsley and scallions between the bowls and mix well.

❷ Preheat the oven to 400°F/200°C. Keep the phyllo pastry sheets covered with plastic wrap to prevent them from drying out. Take a sheet of phyllo, brush with melted butter, then place a second sheet on top. Cut into 4-inch/10-cm squares. Place a teaspoonful of the salmon mixture on each square. Brush the edges of the pastry with melted butter, then draw together to make little pouches. Press to seal. Repeat with 2 more sheets of phyllo and the salmon mixture, then repeat with the remaining sheets of phyllo and the crabmeat mixture.

❸ Lightly oil a cookie sheet and place the parcels on it. Bake in the preheated oven for 15 minutes until golden. Serve warm.

Devils & Angels
On Horseback

Tempting morsels to bring out the devil in you and raise the party spirit, these are delicious, classic snacks on a stick.

makes 32

Devils	Angels
8 rindless lean bacon strips	8 rindless lean bacon strips
8 canned anchovy fillets, drained	16 smoked oysters, drained if canned
16 blanched almonds	
16 no-soak prunes	

Method

❶ Preheat the oven to 400°F/200°C. For the devils, cut each bacon strip lengthwise in half, and gently stretch with the back of a knife. Cut each anchovy fillet lengthwise in half. Wrap an anchovy half around each almond and press them into the cavity where the stones have been removed from the prunes. Wrap a strip of bacon around each prune and secure with a wooden toothpick.

❷ For the angels, cut each bacon strip lengthwise in half and gently stretch with the back of a knife. Wrap a bacon strip around each oyster and secure with a wooden toothpick.

❸ Place the devils and angels on a cookie sheet and cook in the preheated oven for 10–15 minutes until sizzling hot and the bacon is cooked. Serve hot.

San Francisco Wings

Chicken wings cooked in a wonderfully sticky, slightly spicy sauce never fail to please. You can serve the wings hot or warm.

makes 12

5 tbsp dark soy sauce

2 tbsp dry sherry

1 tbsp rice vinegar

2-inch/5-cm strip of orange rind, pith removed

juice of 1 orange

1 tbsp light muscovado sugar

1 star anise

1 tsp cornstarch, mixed to a paste with 3 tbsp water

1 tbsp finely chopped fresh gingerroot

1 tsp chili sauce

3 lb 5 oz/1.5 kg chicken wings

Method

❶ Preheat the oven to 400°F/200°C. Place the soy sauce, sherry, vinegar, orange rind, orange juice, sugar, and star anise in a pan and mix well. Bring to a boil over a medium heat, then stir in the cornstarch paste. Continue to boil, stirring constantly, for 1 minute, or until thickened. Remove the pan from the heat and stir in the ginger and chili sauce.

❷ Remove and discard the tips from the chicken wings and place the wings in a single layer in an ovenproof dish or roasting pan. Pour the sauce over the wings, turning and stirring to coat.

❸ Bake in the preheated oven for 35–40 minutes, turning and basting with the sauce occasionally, until the chicken is tender and browned and the juices run clear when a skewer is inserted into the thickest part of the meat. Serve either hot or warm.

Spareribs

Terrific to eat but astonishingly messy, so provide plenty of paper napkins. Sticky ribs are easy to prepare and won't keep you away from your guests for long.

makes 30

2 tbsp groundnut or sunflower oil

1 onion, chopped

1 garlic clove, finely chopped

1 fresh green chile, seeded and

finely chopped

3 tbsp clear honey

2 tbsp tomato paste

1 tbsp white wine vinegar

pinch of chili powder

⅔ cup chicken stock

1 lb 12 oz/800 g pork spareribs

Method

❶ Preheat the oven to 375°F/190°C. Heat the oil in a heavy-based pan over a medium heat. Add the chopped onion, garlic, and green chile and cook, stirring occasionally, for 5 minutes until softened. Stir in the honey, tomato paste, white wine vinegar, chili powder, and stock and bring to a boil. Reduce the heat and simmer, stirring occasionally, for 15 minutes until thickened.

❷ Meanwhile, chop the spareribs into 2-inch/5-cm lengths and place in a roasting pan. Pour the sauce over them, turning and stirring to coat. Roast in the preheated oven for 1 hour, turning and basting with the sauce frequently, until the ribs are thoroughly browned and sticky.

❸ Remove from the oven, transfer to a warm serving dish, and serve immediately.

Indonesian Peanut Fritters

These crisp bites are so effortless that you can cook them when the party is in full swing. Equally, you can prepare them in advance and quickly reheat in the oven when required.

makes 20

¼ cup rice flour

½ tsp baking powder

½ tsp ground turmeric

½ tsp ground coriander

¼ tsp ground cumin

1 garlic clove, finely chopped

½ cup unsalted peanuts, crushed

½–⅔ cup coconut milk

salt

groundnut oil, for frying

Method

❶ Combine the rice flour, baking powder, turmeric, coriander, cumin, garlic, and peanuts in a bowl. Gradually stir in enough coconut milk to make a smooth, thin batter. Season to taste with salt.

❷ Pour the oil into a heavy-based skillet to a depth of about ½ inch/1 cm and heat over a high heat until hot. Add tablespoonfuls of the batter to the pan, spacing them well apart, and fry until the tops have just set and the undersides are golden. Turn the fritters over and cook for 1 minute until the second side is golden. Remove with a fish slice, drain on paper towels, and keep warm while you cook the remaining fritters. Serve immediately.

❸ Alternatively, transfer the fritters to wire racks to cool, then store in an airtight container. When ready to serve, place them on cookie sheets and reheat in a preheated oven, 350°F/180°C, for 10 minutes.

Mini Pepperoni Pizzas

Pizzas are always a firm favorite with party guests, and the scone base used here is much quicker and easier to make than a traditional bread dough base.

makes 12

Bases

4 cups self-rising flour,
plus extra for dusting

1 tsp salt

3 oz/85 g butter, diced

1¼–1½ cups milk

olive oil, for greasing

Pepperoni topping

¾ cup ready-made tomato
pizza sauce

4 oz/115 g rindless bacon, diced

1 orange bell pepper, seeded and chopped

3 oz/85 g pepperoni sausage, sliced

½ cup grated mozzarella cheese

½ tsp dried oregano

olive oil, for drizzling

salt and ground black pepper

Method

❶ Preheat the oven to 400°F/200°C. To make the bases, sift the flour and salt into a bowl, add the butter, and rub it in with your fingertips until the mixture resembles bread crumbs. Make a well in the center of the mixture and add 1¼ cups of the milk. Mix with the blade of a knife to a soft dough, adding the remaining milk if necessary.

❷ Turn out on to a lightly floured counter and knead gently. Divide the dough into 12 equal pieces and roll out each piece into a round. Place on a lightly oiled cookie sheet and gently push up the edges of each pizza to form a rim.

❸ For the topping, spread the tomato sauce over the bases almost to the edge. Arrange the bacon, orange bell pepper, and pepperoni on top and sprinkle with the cheese. Sprinkle with the oregano, drizzle with a little olive oil, and season to taste with salt and pepper.

❹ Bake in the preheated oven for 10–15 minutes until the edges are crisp and the cheese is bubbling. Serve immediately.

Mini Artichoke Pizzas

This recipe offers an alternative, equally tempting topping for the simple scone base featured on page 88. Make a mixed batch for a colorful addition to your party buffet.

makes 12

Bases

4 cups self-rising flour,
plus extra for dusting

1 tsp salt

3 oz/85 g butter, diced

1¼–1½ cups milk

olive oil, for greasing

Artichoke topping

¾ cup ready-made tomato
pizza sauce

½ cup dolcelatte cheese, sliced

4 oz/115 g canned artichoke hearts in oil,
drained and sliced

2 shallots, chopped

½ cup grated Gruyère cheese

4 tbsp freshly grated Parmesan cheese

½ tsp dried oregano

olive oil, for drizzling

salt and ground black pepper

Method

❶ Preheat the oven to 400°F/200°C. To prepare the bases, follow Steps 1 and 2 on page 88.

❷ For the topping, spread the tomato sauce over the bases almost to the edge. Arrange the dolcelatte slices, artichoke hearts, and shallots on top. Mix together the Gruyère and Parmesan in a bowl and sprinkle over the pizzas. Sprinkle with the oregano, drizzle with oil, and season to taste with salt and pepper.

❸ Bake in the preheated oven for 10–15 minutes until the edges are crisp and the cheese is bubbling. Serve immediately.

Bruschetta

These savoury Italian toasts taste terrific and can be prepared in advance, ready to pop in the oven when your guests arrive.

makes 30

3 thin ciabatta loaves or baguettes

½ cup green pesto

½ cup red pesto

1 lb/450 g mozzarella cheese, diced

2 tsp dried oregano

pepper

3 tbsp olive oil

Method

❶ Preheat the oven to 425°F/220°C. Slice the loaves diagonally and discard the crusty ends. Toast the slices on both sides under a preheated medium broiler until golden.

❷ Spread one side of each slice of toast with either green or red pesto and top with the mozzarella. Sprinkle with the oregano and season to taste with pepper.

❸ Place the bruschetta on a large cookie sheet and drizzle with the oil. Bake in the preheated oven for 5 minutes, or until the cheese has melted and is bubbling. Remove the bruschetta from the oven and leave for 5 minutes before serving.

Pigs in Blankets

This is a more interesting version of the ever-popular sausages on sticks. For extra variety, use a mixture of differently flavored sausages.

makes 48

16 large, good-quality sausages

4 tbsp Dijon mustard

48 no-soak prunes

16 rindless bacon strips

Method

❶ Cut a deep slit along the length of each sausage without cutting all the way through. Spread the mustard evenly over the cut sides of the slits. Place 3 prunes inside each slit, pressing the sausages firmly together.

❷ Gently stretch each bacon strip with the back of a knife. Wind a strip around each sausage to hold it together.

❸ Cook under a preheated medium broiler, turning frequently, for 15 minutes, or until cooked through. Transfer to a cutting board and cut each "pig" into 3 pieces, each containing a prune. Spear with wooden toothpicks, arrange on a plate, and serve.

Recipe List

- Aïoli *10* • Anchovy, Olive & Cheese Triangles *60* • Baba Ghanoush *22*

- Böreks *52* • Bruschetta *92* • Caribbean Crab Cakes *58*

- Cheese & Apricot Morsels *56* • Cheese & Bean Pâté *30* • Cheese Straws *46*

- Deep-Fried Shrimp Balls *62* • Devils & Angels on Horseback *80* • Easy Nibbles *44*

- Egg & Tapenade Toasties *40* • Filled Croustades *42* • Garlic & Chive Crackers *38*

- Guacamole *16* • Honey & Mustard Drumsticks *72*

- Hummus with Lebanese Seed Bread *20* • Indonesian Peanut Fritters *86*

- Little Feta & Spinach Crescents *54* • Mini Artichoke Pizzas *90*

- Mini Pepperoni Pizzas *88* • Moroccan Pickled Vegetables *50*

- Mushroom & Chestnut Pâté *28* • Pigs in Blankets *94* • Quiche Lorraine *48*

- Quick Chicken Liver Pâté with Melba Toast *24* • Red Bell Pepper Dip *18*

- San Francisco Wings *82* • Sausage Rolls *70* • Seafood Phyllo Parcels *78*

- Sicilian Shrimp *64* • Smoked Fish Pâté *26* • Spareribs *84*

- Spicy Seafood Kabobs *76* • Stuffed Grape Leaves *66* • Taramasalata *14*

- Three-Flavor Pinwheels *36* • Traditional English Potted Shrimp *32*

- Tzatziki *12* • Vegetable Samosas *68*